COLLECTED EXPERIMENTALIS

2005-2008

C000231773

U. G. Világos is a poet, editor, and teacher. His new collection, The *Sensible Archetypes of a God*, is forthcoming in Winter 2023, and a collection of flash-poems titled *Troubles, Nights, Meditations & Memoranda for a Passing Smile* is forthcoming in 2024. He is the editor of *We Still Use Poetry: The 2nd Quarterly Anthology of Contemporary Poetry in the Margins*. He sometimes writes as Discovery Jones. As Jones he has published the poetry chapbook *How to Survive a Shark Attack* and the novels *Possession, 1972.* and *The Last Tracer*.

Also by U. G. Világos

The Lark Sings Wind	(Jenoimissyou Books, 1965)
North of Aries, South of Me	(Esplanade Books, 1972)
Studies in the Vocabulary of Music	(Hyper Atom, 1974)
Water Will Never Cry Me To Sea	(Intodarkness, 1987)
One Long Day, with Optional Returns	(Reticulated Chipmunk, 1992)
There is No Ever So Green Borne Deep	(Hi-Heena Books, 1998)
A Human Melancholy	(Temple Tether, 2007)
The Atomic Fashion Book	(Nebula Nebula, 2012)
Nocturnes	(Tiny Lights, 2022)

Collected Experimentalisms: 2005-2008

U. G. Világos

ISBN: 978-1-915760-36-4

Cover designed by Aaron Kent

Edited & Typeset by Aaron Kent

Broken Sleep Books Ltd
Rhydwen
Talgarreg
Ceredigion
SA44 4HB

Broken Sleep Books Ltd
Fair View
St Georges Road
Cornwall
PL26 7YH

Contents

SPRING

In the vast nothingness of night

I am reminded of
how infinitesimally
small
the nature of grief is

If I push my eyes at a certain angle I can see   two   moons
moving   away   from   us/you.   Everything   has   moved   from   you.

As we hurl

through space,

we clutch our knees

and imagine ourselves

as sentient balls of yarn

buoyed by their own

scientific progress.

The window superimposes me as larger than trees.

I don't like that.

Nobody deserves that.

I've been trying to write the silence of your death.

I want to write the silence of your death.

Your death, so silent.

My grief, so small, so loud.

Every house is a light switch away from a home.

I've been plugging
cords into mushrooms
trying to
trying
trying
trying to
convert bioenergy
of fungi
&
decomposition
into music
you could hear
somewhere in
the vast nothingness of night.

A will only matters if you're alive to see it actioned.

SUMMER

The whirr of carrion into flesh,

the flash of red,

the mole's last act to be redug.

Bat loops * Tkk Tkk bird roosts * Late lethargic butterfly * Lawnmower bee graveyard shift

Paraphernalia of frogspawn shifts

Loose, limp wind solitary

The cows bed down

Cautious cavitation

Doppler fly flies

The banded thief is alone, yelling.

Ultrasound finds the sky's heartbeat as a purr.

Does the earth hum in feline?

Poe's bird shouts once and then

A recursive cry - hedge to hedge

A return in a different pitch.

These things carry on without you.

Why do you not return in a different pitch?

Things you could return as:

3000 tiny gnats waiting to be swallowed
A bat, denied of flight, throwing itself from the second floor
Flying ants stripping their anniversary wings
A nest chewed through from underneath
The Tkk Tkk bird, silent for windchimes
Steel shrinking with a click
A retained bee's single house
A windmill clicking
Poe's birds vocal tennis
A raised wolf announcing itself
Bonfire fresh in midnight air
The stream and the Tkk Tkk bird in harmony

Things you do return as:

Muzzled static

Grief spread across sleep

Tsunami winds

Dreams to ghost and haunt

Nothing. Nothing at all.

AUTUMN

A light flicks off,

                                                        somewhere

a woodpecker

Is wrapping its tongue

around its skull

            I am wrapping my tongue

                around my skull

            I am pressing my teeth

                into my neck

A noise, like a predator's battery, discharges.

Like the memory of you discharging itself.

The heat bites, licks the corners of the sky

My knee pops out I am weakened

A painted red opens its translucent leaves and flies home.

The vampire bird salutes,
returns with another,
returns with another.

Poe's birds harmonise,
a chorus of knocks.

A noise like a gong
anticipating its own impact

Somebody is approaching - a quad bike.

The pram is still out and I have been asked three times.

The cows are bloodcurdled.

I will later learn you never called out.

You.

Alone on the floor.

Alone under the table.

Too proud to cry.

Too far from the Danube to swim home.

Don't forget the eggs

the banded thieves will eat them.

Cows scream / they scream in transport / they scream in knowing

Rain like a round of applause / Shadow of an angel / watching the gutters

drip

WINTER

When you died,
I was promised silence
but I can still hear it all
I can still hear everything
you have contorted to miss.

This grief carries in both sound

in sound

and space

in space

We are back to

silent stream
lights fading
clicking on
f a d i n g
clicking on
m o t i o n

We never spoke about
The bramble's pinch
The translucency of stillness
The sky painted blush
So why would we start now?
Why am I here, approaching nature
for answers from a condition
we never cared to configure.

Finally
an ultrasound
a rumble East to West
tracing the long lost sun
& its immense gravitational pull

Year After Year Onwards

Epilogue

We make our way to morning,
in the corner of the field a nest,
an egg in its throat,
the TKK TKK bird's gallbladder intact.

An Eastern Imperial flies at tree level
as we walk up and down,
a hole in a carrier bag,
your ashes everywhere but here.

This early light is still
bright orange as in a painting
from a time before time,
not forgotten but a mystery

We are in the mud and stones
of the river as somewhere
the day and the dark
meld into one another like time

And then I am in the nest.
The stream is a river,
the mud looks like an ocean.
You are on the banks.

You are in the river, crowing,
heading out to sea once more.
You are reborn, boundless,
a jellyfish again and again.

You are on the river,
with your mother and grandmother
and the water that never stops
to be held with these hands.

The sky and the sea,
the stones and the stars
And you, everywhere,
a crow in a nest catching worms.

It is too difficult to hold this world
in the palms of our hands.
Can we live together today
and die together once more?

LAY OUT YOUR DEEP REST

Milton Keynes UK
Ingram Content Group UK Ltd.
UKHW020604021023
429772UK00008B/41